White Center

White Center

〜〜〜〜〜〜〜〜〜〜〜〜〜〜〜

Poems

by Richard Hugo

W · W · NORTON & COMPANY · INC ·

NEW YORK · LONDON

Some of these poems appeared in the following publications:

Anyart Journal, Esquire, Copperhead, Choice, the *Seattle Review, Northwest Review, Slackwater Review, Ironwood, Slow Loris Press, Graham House Review, Colorado State Review, Chicago Review, Pequod, Field, Southwest Review, Big Moon,* and *Creel.*
The poems "Bay of Recovery" (1974), "The Sandbanks" and "Scene" (1976), "Leaving the Dream" and "Museum of Cruel Days" (1978), copyrighted © in the years shown by The New Yorker Magazine, Inc. Reprinted with permission.
"Birthday," "Graves," "The Small Oil Left in the House We Rented in Boulder," "Belt," and "Beaverbank" originally appeared in *Poetry.*
"Second Chances" originally appeared in *Esquire* magazine.
"To Women," "From Altitude, The Diamonds," and "Doing the House" copyright 1977 by Washington and Lee University, reprinted from *Shenandoah:* The Washington and Lee University Review with the permission of the Editor.

"The River Now" is reprinted from *Pacific Search,* 715 Harrison, Seattle WA 98109.

"High Grass Prairie," "A Good View from Flagstaff," and "Houses" copyright © 1976, 1975, 1976 by The Atlantic Monthly Company, Boston, Mass. Reprinted with permission.

"White Center" reprinted from the *Iowa Review,* Volume 7, Number 1. Copyright © The University of Iowa. Reprinted with permission.

"Fort Benton" and "The Carnival Inside" originally appeared in the *Ohio Review.*

In addition to their appearances in magazines, the following poems appeared in *Road Ends At Tabola,* 1978, Slow Loris Press: "Bay of Resolve," "Bay of Sad Loss," "At the Cabin," "Brief History," and "Fairfield."

The poem, "Port Townsend, 1974," also appeared in *Rain Five Days and I Love It,* 1975, Graywolf Press.

Library of Congress Cataloging in Publication Data

Hugo, Richard F
  White Center.

  I. Title.
PS3515.U3W55   811'.5'4   79–17602
ISBN 0–393–01301–4
ISBN 0–393–00975–0 pbk.
ISBN 0 393 01301 4 cloth edition
ISBN 0 393 00975 0 paper edition

1 2 3 4 5 6 7 8 9 0

For the Wylie Street Writers Association—
Rick, Carole, Naomi, Jim, Lois, Ripley, Matthew, and Melissa

Contents

White Center

Museum of Cruel Days

It's not you, this dead long moan from the past,
the whip coiled, not just for display but to fit tight
in the case. No guard. No guide. You want to feel
a shudder down your neck but the mural is bad,
Serbs tearing Turk horsemen down, Turk swords
flashing, faces screaming louder than any face screams
and softer than April outside in Belgrade where
for all the good good weather and government bring
seasons must go on and someone rule.

These momentos seem ancient. Seem recent.
The woman who brought the key babbled in Serb
though her face was dark Turk and her eyes flashed
a far different smile than her teeth. And you,
alone inside where few tourists come,
you guess the anguish where mace and chain seem
nothing more than old metal. You might have found them
yourself, some afternoon in those pits where you played.
You killed the villain. The girl didn't care.

You hear of anguish. One village nearby, the Germans
shot every male dead in front of mothers and wives.
The count: 7,000. The reason: one captain sniped.
Doesn't that go back further, gratuitous blows
and always the radio on, the indifferent tune?
You scanned the dial days and found no comedian.
You will feel nothing in time. And you can listen
like a hungry dog and not hear the women who cry
'come back' every day at the meadow.

Sweet grim people, some days it hurts, this way
we ought to feel and cannot, this volume of grief

1

that crawls down the ages dissonant in its demand.
A Turk whip is no grain of sand.
That cry for help in the night fell short
of the seawall where you danced and lectured the tide.
You'll remember dull brown this museum's dominant color
and maybe the skin of that woman who waits in the house
next door to lock up after you leave.

Don't come back. Peasants are free and still peasants.
The soil's too rocky to farm. You gather
from some skirmish now going on, the Turks
are ferocious as ever. And if inside you
a fist waits to beat back the bad man you are
that hand opens in hunger. The market opens
and peasants start eating. Not well. Just staying alive.
You're armed with local coin. Buy whatever hunger
looks good on the stand.

After a Train Trip, One Town Remains

If you stopped there it was only to refuel.
Chances are you went by fast and the town curved
by you in the tricky lens the window
of a fast train is. The style: American,
last century farm. The state: someplace high plains.
Much as you like wind on the scene, the vane
didn't move on the water tower. You don't remember
one woman outlined lovingly on sky
or a dog bent hoping someone would want him.

It makes no sense, that town hanging wherever
you are, whatever you do. It reminds you
of nothing, the religion, if anything, grim.
The highest point was the steeple, protestant you think,
for certain not lax. It hovered like a mean bird
over the six homes you counted and you know
if you lived there you'd go to church or be stoned
in the dirt streets Monday, saying hello.

Years later you take the same train. You find
the same town. This time, a tavern, neon
"Grain Belt on tap" in the window and neon cross
on the church. You count nine houses. The market
that must have been there before has macadamed
the parking lot. When you pull out you look back
long as you can. Not very long.

Doing the House

This will be the last time. Clearly
they will tear it down, one slate shingle
at a time and the man here now, last
occupant, face the color of old snow
will leave for the cold he is certain of,
sweating more than last night's bad wine.
He is the man I would have become.
When he leaves he wires the door
and padlocks the wire. When he comes home
he knows his is the one unkept yard
on the block. The weeds, he believes,
are the weeds that will cover his grave.
The style's so old the house does not belong,
not even alone, the way it stood '14
to '44, brush on three sides
not much better, scrub hawthorne
and salal and the dogwood threatening
to die, huge now in some neighbor's
backyard and blooming a white
I don't remember like the walls
yellow as sick eyes inside where I move
room to room, one wall gone, another
for no good reason put up blocking
the kitchen from the room where we ate.
We called it the eating room
and my claim on this has run out.

It's nice of the last man here
to let me come in. I want to tell him
he's me, menial job at the door plant,

table set just barely for one. I want
to tell him I've been writing poems
the long time I've been away and need
to compare them with poems
I left here, never to be written, never
to be found in the attic where hornets
starve and there's no flooring.
Are they wild? Do they ring sad and real
as the years here would have become,
as real and unseen as women
would have been dreamed, curled
in the corner where light still
has a hard time? And later, Lord,
later I would have prayed
and begged to be forgiven for the blood.

This will be the last time. The road
outside's been paved twenty years,
the road no one ever came down
long as I waited, except for a bum
who whistled, "I'll Paint the Clouds
with Your Sunshine." Now the bus
downtown's routed by, every ten minutes
fresh diesel fumes. Across the street
only three of the old homes remain,
one where a sad man lived,
a man who drank himself to the grave
and drank his way into my poems
at least twice. He was the first sad man
I remember. I preferred sadness
to anger and I preferred him
for too long a time. My last gesture
will be at the door, facing east.
It will be a look at the hill

two blocks away, that delayed dawn
every morning and stood between me
and a nation. I live east of that hill.
Thanks to the man with a face the color
of wet salt, the second true sad man
on this block, it is not madness
for the first time I have gone home.

for Philip Levine

Scene

One day at a time. And one barn.
Lovers inside and horses ignoring the lovers.
And the creek nearby. The willows.
That was the scene. I forget the sky.
The sky, let's say, was green
and dotted with silly clouds
that looked like dimes.

Then the horses were lovers.
The lovers had gone to the creek
to celebrate their bones
under the willows and green
under the drifting dimes.
Let's say the lovers were green
and this dream is about them.

And let's say let's say woman and man!
One barn at a time. One moon.
The dimes are dark monsters
ignoring the lovers, the horses
who are also lovers and asleep.
Deep inside deep that is the scene
and I never wake up.

Second Chances

I can't let it go, the picture I keep of myself
in ruin, living alone, some wretched town
where friendship is based on just being around.
And I drink there a lot, stare at the walls until
the buzzing of flies becomes the silence I drown in.
Outside, children bad mouth my life with songs
their parents told them to sing. One showers
my roof with stones knowing I'm afraid
to step out and tell him to stop. Another yells,
"You can't get a woman, old man. You don't get a thing."

My wife, a beautiful woman, is fixing lunch.
She doesn't know I dream these things. She thinks
I'm fine. People respect me. Oh, she knows all right
I've seen grim times. But these days my poems
appear everywhere. Fan mail comes. I fly east
on a profitable reading tour. Once in a while
a young girl offers herself. My wife knows that, too.
And she knows my happiness with her is far more
than I ever expected. Three years ago, I wouldn't
have given a dime for my chances at life.

What she doesn't know is now and then
a vagabond knocks on the door. I go answer
and he says, "Come back, baby. You'll find
a million poems deep in your destitute soul."
And I say, "Go away. Don't ever come back."
But I watch him walk, always downhill toward
the schoolyard where children are playing 'ghost,'
a game where, according to the rules, you take
another child's name in your mind but pretend
you're still you while others guess your new name.

With Ripley at the Grave of Albert Parenteau

He is twice blessed, the old one buried here
beneath two names and a plastic bouquet from Choteau.
He lived his grief out full. From this hill
where Crees bury their dead to give them a view,
he can study the meadow, the mountains
back of mountains, the Teton canyon winding into stone.
I want to say something wrong,
say, this afternoon they are together again,
he and the wife he killed by mistake in the dark
and she forgives him. I don't want to admit
it's cold alone in the ground and a cold run
from Canada with a dog and two bottles of rye.

Say he counted stones along the bottom of the Teton
and the stones counted him one of them.
He scrubbed and scrubbed and never could
rid his floor of her stain.
He smashed his radio and the outside world
that came from it, and something like a radio hum
went on in him the slow rest of his life.
This is the first time I knew his white name.

We won't bring him real flowers this afternoon
jammed with the glitter of lupin and harebells.
This is the west and depth is horizontal.
We climb for a good view of canyons and we are never
higher than others, never a chief like him.
His grave is modern. His anguish goes back—
the first tone from struck rock. You and I,

we're civilized. We can't weep when it's needed or counts.
If you die first, I'll die slow as Big Bear,
my pale days thin with age,
night after night, the stars callow as children.

With Melissa on the Shore

My sudden daughter, grays are latent in that sea.
This moment we turn gull. We ride white spray
over a water sky two freighters ago ignited.
This is where we started, gill and fin and slow scan
of the ocean floor. Waves wiped out all traces
of our birth. No sign of a home, no proof
we ever lived are two insistent grays.

What if the horizon's laughter arrives
over and over, and this thin afternoon it seems
we're little on this beach? What other creature claims
his arms are wings and buzzes the crabs taking cover?
That's one game the dolphin wouldn't dare play.
We fall to the sand tough with laughter. The surf howls
dry disapproval and reads the Bible alone.

Other games matter. Listen. The pound. Here
we face our failure, words we should have said,
anger that spilled over last Tuesday (you don't
remember), the beggar we should have asked in.
The sea is fond of saying that's nothing.
Waves caving on sand say Melissa. The world makes demands
at impossible times and goes on burning with thirst.

And we go on burning. Like water. This is where we
and sky touch each other and tingle. Out there
real gulls clown high over what makes us sad,
that debris we try to forget. Gray is where we start.
What follows the first gray is luck. Look,
that blue's bigger than any sky in Montana.
Foam glows in the dark, white with bones of dead sole.

The Ballpark at Moiese

1

Score tied in the 8th, the only fans, bison
high above the park, turn back to their food.
A home run now, two on, would break the game
wide open. You're anxious in the box.
You pull the trigger on the fifth pitch
and it's over. Over the center fielder's head.
Over the trees in center field. Over moon
and inland gulls, it settles like a dead cloud
on the sleepwalking river
enroute to Japan.
The longest home run ever seen.
Did you see that, bison?

2

These tracks are dead.
Put your ear to them.
You hear no hum of train,
the Polson run that died.
You think of wrong blood
and the anonymous donor.
The Flathead river
moves like luck in sleep.

Men we couldn't find today
even in photos
took that train to Polson
where the lake
laughed blue as girls

and music improved
with each drink.
What that trip meant after
the week's grim labor
and the grimy way they felt
awkward down the track
waving their pay at bison
and the Mission Range.

Money. Fun.
The road takes off to Polson
like a vein.
The train
is on display in Kalispell.

3

Listen. In this dream I am
the only one watching a softball game.
I decide to play one more season.
I go to the home of Ed Schmidt
our first baseman.
His wife, Margaret,
a beautiful woman, greets me at the door.
Ed is out but Ed, she tells me,
will be glad to play again.
I wake up happy,
too old for the game.

4

You were born with wrong blood, saved
by miraculous transfusion. What I'm saying
is accept that blood. After 14 years
it's yours by right of artery and heart.

I should be wise and I'm not. Fifty years
of mistakes and I marry your mother
thinking this time I'll be right. Accept
that blood and dream the anonymous donor.
His hair failed brown. His eyes
beg love in catacombs. His life comes back
event after event in out of way places like Moiese
where he struck out often and made errors.
I should be wise and give blood that others
may dwell on their lives, immediate tingle
of women, the joke that cracked everyone up
that summer in Polson. How did it go?
Know I was right to marry your mother.
Know your blood gains momentum and size
like the river.

5

Crow Creek Reservoir to Dixon.
You can find a thousand spots to picnic.
Even the best ones, grass and shade tree,
ring with something lost. Not tribal ways
of feeling about space. Not some better way
things never were before the white man came.
Red or white, the orphan from Ronan
lives among strange animals
who turn away and graze.

6

What we want to save grinds down finally
to the place it happened, dim charm
of four worn spots we used for bases.
A small boy runs the home run out again

alone in snow. Did you see that, bison?
It comes back often that the river doesn't care
the last game died on the scoreboard.
It comes back once a lifetime
we heard someone cheer.

And what you did that day, score tied,
ignored by bison, the drive
you sent beyond retrieve, you take home
because it cannot mean. Because
it is ignored and lost. Circle the bases again
and claim they speak of it today in Dixon,
the old men in the bar
who were not there,
who every afternoon
take the train that does not run
to Polson anymore.

for Matthew

Wheel of Fortune

One way of going is to bang the door your last time
out of the house, your rage hanging like dangerous gas
on the sun porch where your wife and children are crying.
You send them a postcard from Sweden saying you're sorry
you took all the money out of the bank and you hope
they're not going hungry. You meet a blonde someone
you saw once in a movie and boy is she lovey.
You've taken up painting and already have a dealer
in New York, another in London. Five of your oils
are in European collections and a new museum
in Amsterdam has signed you to a five-year contract.
If it wasn't for one reviewer, a man whose name
sounds a little like the name of your favorite river,
who calls your best shots amateur and once in the *Times*
said you paint like some retarded spastic, you'd really
be happy. You keep his reviews in a scrapbook
and each night sit there reading them over and over
planning his murder. Naturally, you no longer paint.
The museum is suing you. The blonde is having an affair
with Burt Lancaster. Tired and broke you go back home,
the one you slammed out of when this poem began.
You sit there contrite in your rocker and watch TV.
Your wife is cooking your favorite: clam *fettucine*.
The children say you watch too many crime shows,
you ought to take more walks.

Open Country

It is much like ocean the way it opens
and rolls. Cows dot the slow climb of a field
like salmon trawls dot swells, and here or there
ducks climb on no definite heading.
Like water it is open to suggestion,
electric heron, and every moon
tricky currents of grass.

                  Let me guess;
when you repair the damaged brain
of a beaten child or bring to a patient
news that will never improve, you need
a window not a wall to turn to.
And you come back here
where land has ways of going on
and the shadow of a cloud
crawls like a freighter, no port in mind,
no captain, and the charts dead wrong.

for George

The Other Beaverbank

The river seems to sour and we can't recall
who's buried under the mound. We might guess
a name like Poor Bear. We might remember
the sequence: first, the crack of ice,
then tons of drowned bison pouring north,
and finally, for it was spring surely by then,
the crackpot preacher blew his trumpet
loud over the water and swans flew off.
With so much gone, it was natural to sell.

And it's natural to want it back, not just
Beaverbank but the whole wide scene,
the far bank of sand, the three islands
named for Spanish ships and the evening sweep
of falcon counter current. The Missouri
releases and fills like a heart. Some new tenant
we hope will chase some old ghost away
and all swans come home. Surely it's spring:
the cottonwood leaves turn over silver
and flash. We could dig and dig
and find no human remains. The mound?
That was an early joke of settlers.
They knew when they heaped the dirt and stomped it
round like the dome of some early tribe
we'd create the rest years later,
handsome bones and beads,
the sad tale of one who lost it all.

for Mildred

At the Cabin

We ripple aspen the way we move out
in the morning meadow wind. Stay close
through the buffalo willow's manic perfume
across the field of lupin where the fresh track
of a cougar gives us the direction not to go.
We climb high lichen and below us
farther than our first dream of the void
the north fork of the Teton cannot move.
We are frozen deep in hunger.
If we tumble coupled down the rock side
bouncing from the last ledge out in sky
in final isolation like the eagle, like the bones
of Crees, we'll shatter on the valley floor
separate at stars. Love's the best way
to feel safe. Love on moss. Love on springy bed
of juniper. And there must be definite ways
of telling how the mate remaining, widower Mallard
or warrior Cree who killed his wife by mistake
doubles his grief every storm.

Pale letter from home: "We hope you return
someday. We love you still." The pages
ride thermols like white spastic birds
across the canyon to Uninhabited Mountain.
More than letter disappears. More than past.
The red hawk stumbles, catches himself and climbs.
The cougar, spurred by rumor of a spacious cave,
turns south to Ear Mountain and a hoped for role:
I am good enough to own a home.

We come back tired. Ways of hating the past
sour inside us. We bore ourselves remembering
children in ruin, too many tears at the pass.
If the Teton falters, move the rocks.
No matter how water jitters, water
has no nerves. Rivers flow because the first law
of all land is slant. The second, desire to ride.
We ripple aspen the way we move back
to the cabin baking in motionless noon.
And the aspen ring. The river loosens at its pools
and takes off shooting wildly at the sky
like some drunk cowboy, his first night back in town
after centuries of good work done.

Birthday

Wind deserted the pond this morning. The day
aged badly under a single cloud, and birds
abandoned this air where lilies stop waving
and microscum moors to the base of reeds.
Cattails doze under the light's warm weight.
Remember salmon, how they once climbed
over each other frantic to die? Even rivers fade.
Under wings, sudden, out of a birdless north
cars are out of gear and my life runs
empty roads like a sick hand on a map.

Regions beyond worn needs to clown, a man
waits by the road for out-of-date wagons.
The wagons won't come. His children grew weary
calling clouds candy, frying mud on a rock.
They ran from the calendar south. He grows
the same sick corn every year. He tries reading
the girls better ways. Miss August is best,
the least stained by wine he throws at the wall.

If the wind would return, south to north, some
old comforting motion, opening, closing the skies,
letting man peek at the stars and his grave,
I could face those years I lived ashamed
of the demented grocer and his run-down store,
dust on jars, meat dark in the case, the tab
he ran for the poor. I could use the wind
like others use religion, to tell myself
it's ok to be out of rivers and weak.

With wind high, bewildering, I can't imagine
the poor being robbed, an arrest being made.

That fanatic who screamed in the street
about Christ and found cancer her savior—
she's part of my life. On this short day
when air rides green, let's welcome back
with early eyes the shifts of giant bird flocks.
The relentless pour of bruised fish up creeks
that barely trickle and spark, named after miners
the world photoed and lost, who stare at our faces,
their dead eyes hoping for a strike.

for Paul Levitt
with equal shares in December 21

Repairing the House, the Church, Restoring the Music

In early hymns cries came faint
from far off. Someone needed blood.
Money, I said, will make it right.
What I knew seemed echo. The hymns went out
with little hope and came back white as Christ
from tired stars. I admit I faked tears.
Every wrong note hit.
I hated the not meant different shades
of plaster on the walls and the half meant light
in the vestibule. I take on faith
Christ paled from less than loss of blood.

Part of us remains alone. That's good.
All these years I never told a soul about
the thirteenth wren, the first twelve dead.
Take the destitute choir. Isn't it right
given what happened in the interim,
tremoring itself seems firm and walls
whatever color hold out cold.
When tears are real, bad music's not that bad.

I promised myself I'd come back one day
serious about a chapel that cracks
and patches itself with sky
and locate for the first time what we are,
the warm center that has always been,
fireweed that overnight covers the raw dirt
of a meadow cleared by machine.
I kept that promise this morning and, Jesus

or none, stars found their second wind.
These weeds we walk were garden lost
one year to no special music,
music all the same.

for Aunt Sara

Leaving the Dream

Every day became a slow July. Sweat, it was clear,
was what he would do forever. He learned early
women weren't waiting in barns when the workday ended.
It would be wife and children, not much love and no money,
no sun but the one he must labor under,
That's how I saw him, bitter far back in himself.

What did he dream? I dreamed him drunk and alone.
And I dreamed another man younger than him
and strong poking fun when the old one fell in the dirt.
I dreamed he dreamed a hundred bluegill day at a lake
and a cooling wind low in the oak. When my dream grew firm
wild dogs pulled him from my sleep.

You think you've got it? Forget it. That young strong man
I dreamed was not me. The old man had more than one day
of fun. Some good weather repeats. He was more proud
than my dream credits him and he was less sad
than whiskey might make him seem. Besides, when old
no matter how sharp you may limp in some child's crippled
eye.

Lake and slow rivers were home for women with fins.
I've gone back to white creeks with Indian names,
the first promise life makes: it's all downhill and dance.
This time I know better. I can center on the song.
I never dance. Just listen to the band.
The old man sits home caked with day labor and worn.

Last night the young man called the old man a failure.
The old man seemed phoney. He spoke ignorantly

of what the young man knew well, and his weeping seemed
    fake.
I begged, 'Leave him alone. I still love him. He's poor.'
The day moves loud in the leaves like a tremoring past,
some form in the dust, a blinding sky on the way.

Beaverbank

Light from the river brightens your old room.
The heron you called Pete returns still young
to sweep the river like a cloud. This bend's
the one the river loves to make, moving easy
to the bank and curving easy as the moon.
Your eyes ride water and your eyes climb trees.
Nights were filled with horses and each morning
all that final summer twenty years before
beaver crossed in wild herds to the island.
You saved your brother from the undertow.

Call it home when the house you lived in
fades slow as carp swim. The empty house
stands detonative in the sun, tick, tick
of the bomb you left there deafening the ghost.
And it's a sad girl sees that one house lost
to weather and the strange tune starting far back
in the sky and growing as the jobs you held
pile up on your clearance form. The day
your clearance comes declaring now you're eligible
to dream return, a corporation
buys the property and lies about its plans.

Love, I lost that one house too. Long ago.
And I feel nothing now except the faint dream
time to time that had I stayed there
in my makeshift room my poems would still be
personal as doom, ring wild with fear
until some troubled reader pounded on the door.
I will not answer. I will not go outside

to walk the river. And the beaver when they reach
the island and are safe will not come back
to mind. The deer will not go home.

Go back like you go away, not afraid of loss
and fearful loss will not be there to celebrate
some far off winter when you stumble on
the ruins, your eyes downriver gray.
Your fear means you lose nothing. Your brother
has four children, and the current rides
in such firm ways no map gets out of date.

for Ripley

The Towns We Know and Leave Behind, The Rivers We Carry with Us

I forget the names of towns without rivers.
A town needs a river to forgive the town.
Whatever river, whatever town—
it is much the same.
The cruel things I did I took to the river.
I begged the current: make me better.

Your town, your river, or mine—
it is much the same.
A murdering man lives on the land
in a shack the river birds hate.
He rubs the red shriek of night from his eyes.
He prays to water: don't let me do that again.

Let's name your river: Ohio.
Let's name all rivers one in the blood,
red steam and debris in the blood.
Say George Doty had a wrong head.
Say the Ohio forgives what George did
and river birds loved his shack.
Let's name the birds: heron and sweat.
Let's get away from the mud.

The river is there to forgive the town
and without a river a town abuses the sky.
The river is there to forgive what I did.
Let's name my river: Duwamish.
And let's admit

the river birds don't hate my home.
That's a recent development, really
like mercury in the cod.

Without a river a town abuses the air.
The river is there to forgive what I did.
The river birds hate what I did
until I name them.
Your river or mine—
it is much the same.
A murdering man lived on the bank.

Here's the trick;
We had to stay drunk
to welcome the river
to live in a shack
to die on the bank
beneath the bigoted sky
under the river birds
day after day
to murder away
all water that might die.

A murdering man is dead on the bank
of your new river, The East,
on mine, The Clark Fork.
It is much the same.
Your river has gulls and tugs.
Mine has eagles and sky.
I rub last night from my eyes.
I ask bright water what's happened.

The river, I am not sure which one,
says water has no special power.
What should I do?
Or you?

Now water has no need to forgive
what shall become of murder?
How shall we live
when we killed, when we died by the word?

Whatever the name of the river,
we both had two women to love,
One to love us enough we left behind
a town that abuses the day.
The other to love the river we brought with us,
the shack we lived and still live in,
the birds, the towns that return to us for names
and we give them names knowing the river
murders them away.

for James Wright

Fort Benton

This was the last name west on charts.
West of here the world turned that indefinite white
of blank paper and settlers faded one at a time alone.
What had been promised in Saint Louis proved
little more than battering weather and resolve.
Hungry for women and mail, this town
turned out to watch the Mandan dock.

Church was a desperate gesture, prayer
something muttered bitter. One we called friend
the long Missouri here followed his babble
into the breaks and no one looked for his bones.
We still don't look for friends who turn into air.
Given the right seed and seasonal luck
a love of land becomes a need for each other.

The river slides into the breaks. Nothing comes back,
man, Mandan, the latest word on sin.
Trains killed boats and died in their turn.
Where we look deep the river smirks.
Let's recognize 'hello there' and 'nice day'
spare us those improvements that give way
beneath us like the bank someday for sure.

The best towns, no matter how solvent, seem
to barely hang on. This is the town to leave
for the void and come back to needing a home.
It may be the aged river or the brick hotel
on the bank, heavy as water, or the ritual
that shouldn't be hard to start: the whole town out
shouting 'come back' at the breaks one day a year.

for Jan

32

High Grass Prairie

Say something warm. Hello. The world
was full of harm until this wind
placated grass and put the fish to rest.
And wave hello. Someone may be out there
riding undulating light our way.
Wherever we live, we sleep here
where cattle sleep beside the full canal.
We slept here young in poems.
The canal runs on without us east
a long flow into Fairfield. The grass flows
ever to us, ever away, the way it did
that war we dreamed this land alive.
The man we hoped was out there
saw our signal and is on the way.
Say something warm. Hello. You can sleep
forever in this grass and not be cold.

Brief History

Dust was too thick every summer. Every winter
at least one animal died, a good friend,
and we forgot the burial ritual after our Bible
washed away in the flood. We mumbled anything
that occurred to us over the grave. Finally
only our wives were left to hate, our children
who ran off to Detroit and never came back.
How we raged at change, the year the ground
went fallow, the time our wheat grew purple
and the government couldn't explain. Less fish
in the lake every year, grain prices falling
and falling through dark air, the suicide bird
who showed us the good way out. The century
turned without celebration. We tried to find fun
in the calendar, the strange new number, nineteen.
It was women held us together. They cautioned
us calm the day we shouted we knew
where millions in diamonds were buried
and ran at cattle swinging the ax.
We forget that now. We are planning hard
for the century ahead.

Medicine Bow

This is the way the road bent then, wide and sullen
across baked earth and I was with two bums
I'd picked up outside Meeteesee. That was a day
I thought being kind was important because the world
that summer was dust and rejection, and banners
of welcome in Red Lodge hung limp. I was drunk.
Heat soured the sky. The day would come I vowed
when I would fight. I bought a room for the bums.
The next day I gave them both money in Loveland
and waved goodbye and drove off smug as the rich.

How many years ago was that? What songs played out
miles of what should have been, on whatever station
the radio found leaking through acres of cactus?
What happened that day in Medicine Bow? Sudden snarl
of the woman running the motel. The knife I kept
under my pillow that night, convinced that here
at last I'd found the source of all evil, the final
disgrace, world ending a way no poet predicted.

My Buick was yellow then. This one is green and zips
to Laramie easy. The whole business that day
in Medicine Bow and Medicine Bow seem silly.
It may not have been here at all. The brown block
hotel seems familiar, but it may be the road, the way
it bends into town is wrong. Denver stations
are coming in clear and that time I got nothing.
When you drive fast, hay seems to fly.

Overlooking Yale

Top Of The Park, Hillis. Top of the World.
Long Island Sound bounces a gold ball
of dawn off a reflective glass building
(the firm inside bankrupt) and it lands on The Green.
The Green lies white in ice
and out of sermons. I am out of wisdom,
eating French toast cooked the year
Yale was founded, too timid to complain,
too far from home to trust my manners.
I'm sure I'm being observed
and my act is not clean. Western paranoia.
John Wayne. Three centuries short
of history. One of stability. Way ahead
in weather and rustic charm you can't trust.
With Yale below in gold light, I feel
I should have read Milton, ought to be
in the know about something, some key remark
Dryden made about Donne. Not concerned
with the way we talk to old cars,
pat their hoods and murmur "sweet hero."
Two hundred thousand miles and only
five changes of oil and one valve grind.
I should try for salvation but below
the three chapels lock tight as a witchburner's heart.
Out west, survival is enough. Here,
the lone gull that hides in the sun
like a World War II fighter plane
and dives on the small shop below, the one
with a sign I can read, "Living Things,"
has no stature after the raid, perched

puffy and proud on the grotesque K of C building
awaiting a drum roll and the DFC.
And you'd best not trust either the warm way
light looks filling the streets, nor warm looks
on student faces when you make a major point.
They'll remember you wrong in time,
your point will be perverted to their purpose
and all purpose is impure. I remember
what I do for nothing and no reason fondly,
staring New Haven away and in its place
a garden from way back and the sweat
of those who could barely read and write,
bent to immediate weeds, first sprout
of carrot, promise of lettuce and bean,
all the way across this nation,
and inside the house, four books counting
The Bible and all but The Bible long
out of print. And I don't feel I have come
so very far from that. Top Of The Park.
Top of the World. The limousine leaves soon
for New York and the plane, the plane for points west.
For sure we die at either end of the run.
For the first time the east is not the east
dreamed from a hill on the edge of Seattle.
Give that gull his medal.
When you see a ghost, try to be nice.

for Hillis Miller

Imagining Delaware

When I imagine Delaware
I see a lonely canal,
a lock gate stuck half open,
water crawling out slow foam.
I see a man
also lonely, and grieving.
I am not sure why.
If it's Monday
the sky's a promissory green.
Later in the week
the sky's grim white.

I'm speaking our time,
the time I imagine.

The man keeps his face turned.
It's hard to tell he's grieving,
to see his tears for sure.
Once in a great while, a woman,
not invited, not from Delaware
(I imagine no Delaware women)
passes between me and him.
I want to imagine more,
not let the scene end there,
the shadowy woman gone,
the man still turned,
the sky by now heavy
with threat of night.
Dog or dinosaur,
I want something more.

I've never been in Delaware.
It must be something like that,
however it's put,
soft 'pass away,' hard 'die.'

A Good View from Flagstaff

Let's take it as it is: acres flowing
yellow north and people so small in the distance
we believe them happy working fields.
Despite the heat, the sun is less than cruel.
Soil is wet black and the wheat rolls far enough
to be a lemon sea. Silos waver
and are silver salmon two wines into lunch.

This view is what one needs to love the world
when things go bad. Take Naples, '67, me alone
in Vomero, no sleep for nights, endless sweat,
my system out of chemical whack from weeks
of suicidal drinking and the sad scenes of my life
locked with me in the hotel room like bats.
Far off, through my window, a white apartment
building gleamed each morning and I knew
out there beyond me somewhere was a world
worth having because it caught the sun
and sent the light back to the sea confirmed.
Because it sat there quiet far away.

A good view here. We ignore the mean acts
in the houses though we can't forget they go on
daily with the soul's attrition. We are certain
why the plowhorse limps. Spread the way it is
by wind, the world in cultivated patchwork
claims we travel on the right freight one day
and the years are gone. At worst
they're more than nothing. The best friends
we remember took us home the way we are.

Port Townsend, 1974

On this dishonored, this perverted globe
we go back to the sea and the sea opens for us.
It spreads a comforting green we knew when children—
celery—Wesson Oil can—through islands. It flares
fresh immediate blue beyond the world's edge
where dreams turn back defeated and the child weeps
replaying some initial loss. Whatever it does for us
it is resolute, even when it imitates sad grasses
on the inland plains and gulls are vultures overhead
hidden in the bewildering glare.
Aches of what we wanted to be and reluctantly are
play out in the wash, wash up the sand and die
and slip back placid to the crashing source.
The sea releases our rage. Logs fly over
the seawall and crush the homes of mean neighbors.
Our home, too. The sea makes fun of what we are
and we laugh beside our fire, seeing our worst selves
amplified in space and wave. We are absurd.
And sea comes knocking again in six hours. The sea
comes knocking again. Out there, salmon batter
candlefish senseless for dinner. The troller flashes
his dodger through the salmon school. The sky widens
in answer to claustrophobic prayer. The sea believes us
when we sing: we knew no wrong high back in the mountains
where lost men shred their clothes the last days
of delirium and die from white exposure. We found one
sitting erect, his back against the stars, and even dead
he begged us to take him west to the shore of the sea.

Getty

Today, I remembered Getty, the old man
at Price's lake who rented boats and coughed
and told me he was gone. Moss caked his lungs
and a sky I'd forgotten drifted in his eyes.
The brooks I caught were dazzling and wild.
I shouted 'Lord love Getty' at the trees.
Nothing came back. The young sheen of willows
hung over cedars dark and grumpy with age.

I came back early next spring but Getty
prophetically blue, had gone, that winter
I stayed home in Seattle and wrote hard
to make 'alive' and 'violent' do for the sky.

Some days the fish don't bite. You know that.
And we die at wrong times, like Friday.
Whatever day Getty died, it could not be special
or wrong, an old man like him, alone
with a lake, no urge to go after trout
and no particular feeling when nylon
arcs out over the water, hangs that one moment
all moments pulse, first kiss, first soft light
in the eyes of the girl who seemed nothing last week,
and settles soft as a far teal
and waits.

Let's see. What happened today: a mild fight
in the tenure meeting. We voted nine to one 'no.'
A disturbed student raged in my office
about elk roaming some desert for water.
A swim—I felt my arms harden

and knew I was building more wind.
On the way home, night ignited the town
and I thought of a speech: In conclusion,
let me say Getty let me say—
I remembered his eyes and the sky in them,
his easy prediction coughed out
like we had plenty in common.

The Small Oil Left in the House We Rented in Boulder

That's a place I've been. The town
small across the river and compact. Two women
gather salad cress. Two men chat on the far bank.
No doubt May—flowers flaring, quiet river high
and no doubt nothing more than the tree in bloom
goes on. I didn't want to live there then.
I want to live there now and not go mad.
I still believe there was a time I could.

It must have been enough to see the buildings
double in the river, to know that roadless world
where you go nowhere ever and the old
pass wisdom down, time of day for pike, time
of moon for planting, time to die and float away.
And since the world stops where the river bends
from sight, the body must pass on to some place
warm in the minds of children though they have
no word for heaven and the hot wind reeks.

Orofino, Idaho, is close, but wrong.
For one thing, there's a bridge, and one day
moments after a child had drowned, I drove by
on my way to Portland, past the frantic divers
and the wailing mother, and I kept going,
concentrating on the radio, the tune playing,
"Adios," oh lovely, from the local station.
That was May and God the river roared.

At Our Best

Face the moon. Ask: is it less, now that man
has been there? That's what some claim. They say
we've dirtied that gleam and lovers must look
elsewhere for support, Venus or the stars
burned out, burning with illusion like all love.
We kill our wives to have the other woman.
When wives die they fix us in their final stare.
Their eyes ask why. We turn away ashamed.
We move to the country where the nearest law
and telephone are miles beyond the humorless rim
of the mountains and we beat our dogs at dawn.
Their howls can't reach even the next farm.
Their eyes ask why. We move back to the city.
Our lives are sodden on our backs. We shuffle
alley to alley alone, mumbling thanks
for a dime we know's devalued like the moon.
Once, beached by storm, we found a shark jaw
polished by tide, light from China, sand.
We shouted, "We are wealthy," at the moon.
No confirming word came back. Only the level wind
slanting our fire east and we leaned west
against direction and sang. We didn't care
our words lived less than a moment in sky.

Graves

The flat year, when summer never arrived
grass lived green to August and we buried love
under the grass and marked the grave with a stick.
Wherever we went that fall, Mexico City,
Istanbul, we vowed to go back next year
and dig love up, resurrect love, make love
something for the ages. We planned disciples
and a book big as the Bible. It was all set,
even the witnesses historians believe.

Years later, we found the stick knocked down
by rain, but the spot was certain, there
twelve paces from the apple tree, on a line
with the bay and the anchored freighter
we knew would never move. We dug
and dug. Two moons went by. No love.
We rechecked memory and map and still
only brown dirt and the earthworms twisting away.

We should never have named what we buried.
We know now it wasn't love. Nor a tin can
packed with diamonds. Whatever it was,
dead cat, dead salmon, it flourished
only when skies are odd, when the summer
we expect fails and those abnormal rains
keep the world green longer than the eye takes
to imagine "nothing certain" instead of "love"
on the headstone, rivers fat and trout spawning
year round as if September will not end.

Dwelling

They won't go away, the sea perch
circling piles, the searun cutthroat
hammering home upriver in rain.
I try to ignore them, to focus on women,
on the news. They swim between the lines.
They live in puddles too muddy to see them.
And I see them. They live in dry caves.
They migrate cloud to cloud across
a sky that's always flowing. Bass and catfish,
carp, pompano and cod. What if one day
they were gone? What if all creatures, animal
and man, arrived in some sane ratio?
Would air still stream, light still battle
down tidepools to spot the twenty-ray star?
And would I still feel you cannot die badly
though you scream for mercy and pray
the sky stopped at your door made a mistake?

Changes at Meridian

It's a problem, why I'm here with amplified rock
from the resort hammering the shoreline straight
and driving the planted trout deep where catfish lived
before they were poisoned away. Coves I remember
aren't coves anymore and perch are not welcome
since Fish and Game labeled them scrap. Where I row
the lilies seem decor. No trace of Robert's cabin caving
under the weight of moss. No sunfish nest under the dock.
No old man, set hard in himself, rowing me home.

It's not that no one knows me after forty years
or that at 5 P.M. the surface reflects a world
hopelessly changed for the worse. What nags is
loss of loss, the desperate way I brought farms back
because I wanted the pastures always slanted gently
into the lake, warm reflection of willow and cow,
the old man cautioning patience days the crappie went
        dormant.
These don't come anymore as if I don't need them
and this rehabilitated water, these clustered dull homes are ok.

One poet said it is enough to live perpetually in change.
He didn't believe it. I say we want everything static
including farms we lose and rebuild. That way,
when the fish start feeding and the first chill of day
reminds us we haven't come far, home is a mild row back,
we love the old man repeating over and over,
"Keep your line in the water." Change or no change,
with the right bait this world has twenty-three moons.

Guns at Fort Flagler

Some foreign freighter crawls a blue path north
to Juan de Fuca and we let it go.
We didn't used to. All who entered here,
this passage between Marrowstone and Whidbey,
were invaders and we made them pay.
We pointed these black cannons at them
and we shouted 'boom'
and they came coughing foam, hands high in surrender.

That was forty years ago, the real war
still to come. We believed citations,
the distinguished cross of heron over smelt,
adoring women, the deep meaning of taps
across the water sad on a minus tide,
flag at half mast and roses floating where the hero
took his green chill place among the ratfish.
Three wars later, one win, one tie, one loss,
the guns never fired hang limp in their mounts.

Any war could be called off because of weather.
Rain's not good for ammo and one glint of sun deflects
confident rounds off target. The alert goes out:
salmon in the camp! and candlefish close ranks.
Danger below the surface it is wise to know
how silly we look in uniform saluting the ship
that passes too far out to tell us where it's from,
has no interest beyond instrument readings and charts
that help it through the straight, then help it cross
the blank enormous water, the only check point
music from the port picked up days out.

Fairfield

"A guy I used to know—he taught me all about the sky."
Humphrey Bogart in *High Sierra*

I wanted it depressed, one dusty road
and two cafés both with 'help wanted' signs.
Where I ate, the waitress was too in love
with the cook for things I wanted to say.
The canal passed through town ripe green
and grain, I had to admit, grew assured.
A dog slept fat on warm gravel. No trouble foreseen
raising funds to build the new gym.

I'd expected hurt, the small town kind everyone
knows and ignores, a boy who tried and tried
to leave home, sobbing his failure alone
at the mirror back of the bar, still wearing
his '39 letter sweater, still claiming
the girl who moved to Great Falls will return.
I wanted to honor him in this poem,
to have the sky turn dark as I drove off,
the town in my rear view mirror
huddled with fear white in black air.

The drunk I saw seemed happy. I drove empty away.
What if Fairfield sent signals to Mars
and signals came back saying all weather is yours
no matter how vulgar? I imagined cruel sky
left every bird orphan. When I passed
Freeze Out Lake I saw herons accepted that refuge
as home, and I knew the water was green with sky,
not poisoned green with resolve.

To Women

You start it all. You are lovely.
We look at you and we flow.
So a line begins, on the page, on air,
in the all of self. We have misused you,
invested you with primal sin. You bleed
for our regret we are not more.
The dragon wins. We come home and sob
and you hold us and say we are brave
and in the future will do better.
So far, so good.

Now some of you want out and I don't
blame you, not a tiny bit. You've caught on.
You have the right to veer off flaming
in a new direction, mud flat and diamond mine,
clavicord and dead drum. Whatever.
Please know our need remains the same.
It's a new game every time, one on one.

In me today is less rage than ever, less hurt.
When I imagine some good woman young
I no longer imagine her cringing
in cornstalks, cruel father four rows away
beating corn leaves aside with a club.
That is release you never expected
from a past you never knew you had.
My horse is not sure he can make it
to the next star. You are free.

How to Use a Storm

Where did the storm come from? No warning
on the forecast and no warning wind.
We'd put off putting the storm windows on
and insulating the attic when
bang, rain on glass, and now we can't name
the brown form cringing under the cutbank.
Trees go wild in protest and dogs crawl
sullen into the past. All plans are off.
One cloud covers the world pole to pole.

In these moments, each to his life and each
alone in himself. I ride rough water
under dark skies more than forty years back.
My cousin is rowing. I am going to die.
I am alone on a prairie
waving hello to bison miles off and blind.
Men work hard in a barn. Because I'm open
and warm they disdain me. Women
disdain me because I warp in their glare.

The storm is over. The brown form under
the cutbank's a badger. What hope's open
to him? He makes us sick
the way he near slithers, his hair wet
and flat like a villain's, his every motion
faintly intestine. We say wherever
he lives it's not fit for others.
Sun fills our kitchen. Tamaracks ask
for this dance and dogs beg food at our door.

The trouble with weather, what's happening now
we think will go on forever.

Moments are slower than days.
Between storms, we believe our weather ideal,
our home safe from those we can't stand.
Better we plan our kitchen to trap
whatever light arrives, and whatever creature
huddles in the blue, a storm's a good time
to remember home is where he says hello.

How Meadows Trick You

I said the glint was thistle. It turned out tin.
The place had a history of picnics.
Include the last sad hour, others left for home,
paper scattered, the long long angle of sun.
In games, children took turns dying
in the run-down barn, and whatever animal
roared in the woods that ringed the meadow,
in time he grew tame, his roar was part of the play.

And what would it matter now if I found it,
was reassured it all happened once, even
the women who, given these years, I'm convinced
I invented. Or was that earlier, in snow
where I'd fallen and one was smiling above me
saying her name: Laurie Roy? That can't be.
I used to remember everything that happened
plain as the love on her face. Now it mixes
and fades. A jungle. A blistering day
in the desert. Typhoon. The Taranto docks.
Grim G.I.'s on the ship sailing west.

If I say thistle and the glint is tin
and picnics never happened, you can believe
something in me is modern. I am no longer
always the last to leave. When I find that meadow
I love and drive off certain some places remain,
I take stock of the light. You can believe the dark
on its way and the durable women
who hover ahead of your car and pilot you home.

Snow Poem

To write a snow poem you must ignore the snow
falling outside your window.

You must think snow, the word as a snotty owl
high on the telephone pole

glowering down and your forehead damp with fear
under the glare

of the owl who now is mating. On rare days
we remember the toy

owl we buried under the compost heap,
white sky passing above, warm chirp

of wren and the avenging hawk.
That was summer. Let us go back

to snow and forget that damn fool lecture
I gave last winter.

Well, then: here is your window.
The storm outside. Outside, the dead dove drifting.

The Carnival Inside

I went timid to that town
where banners welcomed strangers and the mayor
sang halleluiah in the park. It was warm and foreign.
All I knew seemed shaken, long days of toil
in heat and the petulant river carping
at the edge of the field, grim moon. The town band
played such lively tunes, I danced.
The first time.

I said, I'll never go back.
Then Sunday and the music died.
I asked what's wrong. This is the day for worship,
not fun, the police explained. On this day
we give thanks for fun. We honor land
and the food it grows. Boys give thanks for girls,
girls boys, and so on. I stood empty in the empty square.
That won't happen again.

I went home sad. I said
you interrupt music for purpose you are dying.
I went on working, sun and river the same.
Once I started back alone to town. A man along
the road said the town had been destroyed.
I sing in the fields and I've decked the scarecrow
in satin. The moon is a grand comedian.
I laugh so hard I hurt.

From Altitude, the Diamonds

You can always spot them, even from high up,
the brown bulged out trying to make a circle
of a square, the green square inside the brown,
inside the green the brown circle you know is mound
and the big outside green rounded off by a round line
you know is fence. And no one playing.

You've played on everyone. Second base somewhere
on the Dallas Tucson run, New Mexico you think,
where green was brown. Right field outside Chicago
where the fans went silent when you tripled home
the run that beat their best, their all-season
undefeated home town Sox. What a game you pitched
that hot day in the Bronx. You lost to that left hander,
Ford, who made it big, one–nothing on a fluke.
Who's to believe it now? Fat. Bald. Smoking your fear
of the turbulent air you are flying, remembering
the war, a worse fear, the jolting flak, the prayer.

When air settles, the white beneath you opens
and far below in some unpopulated region
of whatever state you are over (it can't be Idaho,
that was years ago) you spot a tiny diamond,
and because you've grown far sighted with age
you see players moving, the center fielder
running the ball down deep, two runners
rounding third, the third base coach waving hard
and the hitter on his own not slowing down
at second, his lungs filled with the cheers of those
he has loved forever, on his magnificent tiny way
to an easy stand-up three.

Bay of Sad Loss

For fifty years the bubbles marked
where the ship went down. The romantic one,
sails like summer clouds, the lusty "land ho"
from the crow's nest and the cheering on deck.
Wild times, looking back. We study
the blue sweep of the bay over a vodka tonic.
Remember the albino blue shark we took
off Chile and gave to the zoologist in Vis?

Didn't we burn once, burn in the glare
of sea, in the winds we dreamed, the women
we dreamed in those winds, over our
geography lesson (why was China yellow?)
insects humming outside, prop plane humming
the warm day open, girl in the warm dream
saying "Go to Iceland. Come back and I'm yours."

And what the hell happened? What went wrong
1927? The captain who issued
soft bizarre orders. The first mate suddenly
sobbing and screaming, "It makes no matter.
It makes no matter at all." We sailed
into this bay, our cargo damaged by storm
and said we'll try it again. One more time.
And we still say it. The weather station
gets better predicting the wind.

Bay of Resolve

Think how we touch each other when we sight land
after two years at sea. How we say, "It's still there."
The gulls weren't lying who came to pilot us home.
No matter what happens inside them, the houses climb
lovingly tight to hills, and the smoke rising
above the houses takes the sea chill out of our bones.
When we make out women, the form of them certain
against the white seawall, we stand on the rail and wave.

What holds us back? The shore boats are waiting.
We sit glum in our quarters and sweat. The mate
yells, "going ashore" and the pink girls in the corner
with wild lemon hair cry "farewell," our bite marks
still clear on their necks. How they fought for our kisses
south of Australia. What dishes they cooked.
Can we ever leave them? Those bright days they flew
ahead of the bow singing "on," every red inch
of their bodies stung by the shark spray, their faces
shining alive with our love under the pulsing sky.
Our first kiss on land is cold. We turn away.

This bay never gets wild. The harbor is ideal. We need
not anchor our boat. Three months of summer
the water lies flatter than dawn. In this calm weather
we have no reason to mock the captain or sneak
back of the bilge pump to study worn photos of girls.
Long ago, didn't we read how all journeys end?
The man in that story, his name lost now, came home
tired from the raw world of dragon and flame
and developed a coin, still in use, a salmon on one side
under the words "Good As Water." On the other
a woman firm in silver relief.

Bay of Recovery

This water started it all, this sullen arm
of gray wound loose about the islands
whipped in patches by the north wind white.
The girl on the cliff exposed her body
to wind and whispered "whip me whip me."
I was less than bird, awkward on my bad leg,
half drunk from last night, and maybe
you don't think I'm telling it all.
                              All right.
There was this sullen girl in tight pants
on the shore who whispered "love me"
at the stumps of broken pile.
                              All right.
There was this girl I could barely make out
alone in moonlight on a passing ship.
Sequins, I am sure. Even now I see the sparkle
of her skin.
            No. No. Let me try it again.
There was no girl and I was in good shape.
This water started it all, the dazzling arm
of blue blue promise and the dazzling gull.
Gull. Not girl. And it was less than dazzle,
it was more than being alone on the beach
young under the moon, started it all.

The Sandbanks

We went to the moon those empty Sundays,
air purple with chill. Once, we found
the jawbone of a horse. Another time, a creek
no one had heard of, a creek without a name
and that close to home. And though the cliff
had been cut by man, and first avenue south
was near, we were the first men there.

I remember it cold. Cold strata of sand
and cold fern. The mysterious cold air
that hung in the pit. The cold rim
of the sandbanks above us. Cold sky.
I remember the way the nation broke east
yellow and cold, and the Cascades
hiding the nation, snow and blue stone.

I took the jaw home. Where have you been?
There's a way of knowing why we go
to places others pass by. It has to do
with water we discover and bones.
It has a lot to do with rehearsal,
having the right lines to say in that country
we may find ourselves, the grass
in despair and no one friendly in sight.

The River Now

Hardly a ghost left to talk with. The slavs moved on
or changed their names to something green. Greeks gave up
old dishes and slid into repose. Runs of salmon thin
and thin until a ripple in October might mean carp.
Huge mills bang and smoke. Day hangs thick with commerce
and my favorite home, always overgrown with roses,
collapsed like moral advice. Tugs still pound against
the outtide pour but real, running on some definite fuel.
I can't dream anything, not some lovely woman
murdered in a shack, not saw mills going broke,
not even wild wine and a landslide though I knew both well.
The blood still begs direction home. This river points
the way north to the blood, the blue stars certain
in their swing, their fix. I pass the backwash where
the cattails still lean north, familiar grebes pop up,
the windchill is the same. And it comes back with the odor
of the river, some way I know the lonely sources
of despair break down from too much love. No matter
how this water fragments in the reeds, it rejoins
the river and the bright bay north receives it all,
new salmon on their way to open ocean,
the easy tug returned.

Sound Track Conditional

Say you're drunk or drugged and something hums
far off. A factory. A storm. The sound
reminds you how you thought life would be,
Fresno, alone, thirty years back
on a mountain outside town, green valley
flaring away below you like a tune, Oberon's
slow death in *Wuthering Heights*.
You think about time, how your life runs down
one year each day of passing sky.
Clouds tear overhead. A woman dead
is a lot of women, starting with cranes.

Say you're clear and sober and something hums
far off. A carousel. A flume. The sound says
you keep dying like a song and being revived.
The sound says you keep being reviewed
like a movie hit, the critics trying to explain
huge crowds across the land. What to Butte
says something vital also to New York?
Perhaps the killing at the end. You want
her dead after the rotten things she did.
No. That was El Paso and the mongoloid
in the sideshow frowned and batted her beads.

Say this: you're living alone and the hum
has stopped. Ten years of silence. Ten years
of hammering reruns and your cry
directed at no one morning to night.
You cook enough soup to live through July.
You phone every day. Old films projected

on your wall are grainy and jerk. You can't sleep.
Then, one morning, the hum starts. You run
to the door and shout at the sky, "I'm here."
Dead women hum alive on your lawn.
The sky slows down. You win thirty more years.

Belt

I had been on the road before. The first time
in a foreign land. Dead men lay along the side
and a woman sobbed. She offered me wine
and said one was her son. I understood
though I didn't know the tongue, a wild
gutteral grunt that turned the top soil gray.
That language was so harsh there were no trees.
I must have been ten. And I must have it wrong.
No record anywhere. No war in the world that year.

The town was strange, not like the road. Nothing
in it familiar, not even the humor, the way
the local mechanic kidded the waitress
fresh out of highschool, planning her move
to Great Falls, though I knew every American word,
the good-natured presumption behind the barbs,
and I knew the highschool like it was mine,
main road, movie theatre, hardware, drug store,
the bored girls walking nowhere, the boys
leaving town to go fishing. And I knew here
war was where it belonged, hidden inside
like words I wanted the waitress to say.

And I wanted to call it home, to say to someone,
I lived here before. Where's Al, the grocer?
What happened to his daughter? I drove out
and the sky was livid with hawks. There were flowers
I hadn't seen coming in and the road slanted
a more charming way than it had. White pieces
of cloth left by a surveyor fluttered like flags
of surrender, and the girl I offered a ride got in.
She said, "Wherever you're headed, that's fine."

Bone Hunting

I realized early they were dying like a wall,
the barn they'd never paint again, bird nest broken
and the beaver dam. Skies honored them
by dimming at the burial. Fields back home
went fallow some exact unit of time, day, week,
millennium after the expensive dirt snapped shut
around them and the local creek resumed.
Wind ranted like no one loved the wind.

I buried my love for home, the hard trail
through the woods, the Manards, French
on their porch waving hello when I burst
out of the woods into the paved rich world of car
and turned to the glinting town. I looked at my shoes.
This isn't where the handsome come.
Then the Manards were gone and vivid, the path
wiped out by new housing and I retained every turn.

And what was that movie, Italian, long ago
where a woman died in war in such an offhand way
the crowd thought, 'this means nothing'? The music died
on the sound track. Children ran off chattering to games
and I didn't cry. That's one way to take it: real
and common as rock. Another: to multiply hurt
drink after drink in Las Vegas where showgirls I dream
hint in vain for the key to my room.

I hope I'm right when I say sun gives dirt some odor
it can't find anywhere else in March. A block
from our house, a meadow climbs to a forest
and our dog plays there where my wife and I walk.

Geology says the rock above us will hold
a million more years. We trust that claim
and our dog tearing off like bones are buried
for storage. No shabby reason like song.

Houses

The house you're moving from is not this house
in the sketch, nor that one over there,
your furniture on the porch and your nameplate
weathered fast to the door. The picture's
too idyllic, shade trees rooted strategic and firm,
roses crawling ivy crawling the walls,
leaded windows that double the sadness of rain.
And the real one's too run down. The van
moves off with everything, even the girl
you could not find the courage to ask home.

Some say, 'where I hang my hat.' Some say, 'where
the heart is beating though hurt.' Whatever
you say, make sure it's alone in a cold garage,
the mechanic's hammer banging you mute.
Make sure only you hear the address.
Make sure your car when fixed
will not break down between the home in the sketch
and the home you deny, the boy with your mouth
who shouts goodbye from the roof.

Sail easy on the freeway. Your next home
has never been photoed. Your next home town's where
so little goes on, the hum of your refrigerator
joins the slow river leaving for home.
Isn't it familiar? Rain hitting the south window first?
Dark corner where the warm light can cringe?
If you go with rivers, not roads, the trip
takes longer and you weave and see a lot more.
When you say, 'I live here,' animals
you hadn't thought of for years live on your lawn.
They insist you remember their names.

White Center

Town or poem, I don't care how it looks. Old woman
take my hand and we'll walk one more time these streets
I believed marked me weak beneath catcalling clouds.
Long ago, the swamp behind the single row of stores
was filled and seeded. Roses today where Toughy Hassin
slapped my face to the grinning delight of his gang.
I didn't cry or run. Had I fought him
I'd have been beaten and come home bloody in tears
and you'd have told me I shouldn't be fighting.

Wasn't it all degrading, mean Mr. Kyte sweeping
the streets for no pay, believing what he'd learned
as a boy in England: 'This is your community'?
I taunted him to rage, then ran. Is this the day
we call bad mothers out of the taverns and point them
sobbing for home, or issue costumes to posturing clowns
in the streets, make fun of drunk barbers, and hope
someone who left and made it returns, vowed
to buy more neon and give these people some class?

The Dugans aren't worth a dime, dirty Irish, nor days
you offered a penny for every fly I killed.
You were blind to my cheating. I saw my future certain—
that drunk who lived across the street and fell
in our garden reaching for the hoe you dropped.
All he got was our laughter. I helped him often home
when you weren't looking. I loved some terrible way
he lived in his mind and tried to be decent to others.
I loved the way we loved him behind our disdain.

Clouds. What glorious floating. They always move on
like I should have early. But your odd love and a war

taught me the world's gone evil past the first check point
and that's First Avenue South. I fell asleep each night
safe in love with my murder. The neighbor girl
plotted to tease every tomorrow and watch me turn
again to the woods and games too young for my age.
We never could account for the python cousin Warren
found half starved in the basement of Safeway.

It all comes back but in bites. I am the man
you beat to perversion. That was the drugstore MacCameron
flipped out in early one morning, waltzing
on his soda fountain. The siren married his shrieking.
His wife said, "We'll try again, in Des Moines."
You drove a better man into himself where he found tunes
he had no need to share. It's all beginning to blur
as it forms. Men cracking up or retreating.
Resolute women deep in hard prayer.

And it isn't the same this time. I hoped forty years
I'd write and would not write this poem. This town would die
and your grave never reopen. Or mine. Because I'm married
and happy, and across the street a foster child
from a cruel past is safe and need no longer crawl
for his meals, I walk this past with you, ghost in any field
of good crops, certain I remember everything wrong.
If not, why is this road lined thick with fern
and why do I feel no shame kicking the loose gravel home?